MARCIA
CLARK

MARCIA CLARK

VOICE *for the* VICTIMS

Katherine E. Krohn

Lerner Publications Company • Minneapolis

For Greg Perrin, my vigilant friend

LIBRARY OF CONGRESS CATALOGING-IN-PUBLICATION DATA

Krohn, Katherine E.
  Marcia Clark, voice for the victims / Katherine E. Krohn.
    p.   cm.
    ISBN 0-8225-2892-4 (alk. paper)
    1. Clark, Marcia—Juvenile literature.   2. Public prosecutors—California—
Biography—Juvenile   literature.   3.   Women   lawyers—California—
Biography—Juvenile literature.   I. Title.
KF373.C56K76   1997
345.794'01—dc20
[B]
[347.94051]
[B]   96–16428

Manufactured in the United States of America
1 2 3 4 5 6 – JR – 02 01 00 99 98 97

Contents

At a preliminary hearing in June 1994, Marcia Clark presented evidence linking O.J. Simpson to the murders of Nicole Simpson and Ronald Goldman.

1

The People v. O.J. Simpson

*"You do it because you
have to do it. That's your
job. You go in, and you
protect the people."*
—Marcia Clark

In the still dark, early morning hours of June 13, 1994, Deputy District Attorney Marcia Clark was awakened by the ring of her telephone. The news at the other end of the line was disturbing. Clark's boss, Los Angeles District Attorney Gil Garcetti, informed her that a serious crime had taken place during the night.

Thirty-five-year-old Nicole Brown Simpson, the ex-wife of former football hero O.J. Simpson, had been stabbed to death, along with a friend, 25-year-old

Ronald Goldman. Because Clark was a skilled district attorney and had worked on other high-profile murder trials—crimes that involved celebrities—Garcetti wanted her on the case.

When Clark arrived at Nicole Brown Simpson's condominium at 875 South Bundy Drive, she saw a flock of news reporters outside the home. Behind the canary yellow plastic tape that fenced in the crime scene, Los Angeles Police Department officials collected evidence and snapped photographs. Detectives greeted and briefed Clark. They told her everything they knew about Nicole and Ron on the night of the murders.

The previous evening, Nicole and her family had attended a grade school dance recital. Sydney, Nicole and O.J.'s eight-year-old daughter, had danced in the show. Because O.J. and Nicole were divorced, O.J. had gone to the recital separately.

Later, Nicole and her family, including her mother, Juditha Brown, ate at their favorite Italian restaurant, Mezzaluna, three blocks from Nicole's house. Ron Goldman, a waiter and a friend of Nicole's, was working at the restaurant that night.

After dinner, Nicole treated her children, Sydney and five-year-old Justin, to ice cream at the Ben & Jerry's ice cream shop across the street from the restaurant. Then Nicole and the two children headed home.

O.J. Simpson and Nicole Brown were married in 1985 and divorced in 1992.

At 9:40 that evening, Juditha called Nicole. Juditha explained that she had left her eyeglasses at Mezzaluna. She had called the restaurant manager, who looked around for the glasses and found them. Then Nicole phoned the restaurant and talked to the manager and Ron Goldman. Goldman agreed to drop off the glasses at Nicole's house later that night.

No living person, except the murderer, knows exactly what happened after Ron arrived at Nicole's house. But piecing together a complex puzzle, detectives determined that Nicole and Ron had been killed between 9:45 P.M., when Ron left Mezzaluna, and 10:15 P.M., when a neighbor heard Nicole's white dog, Kato, barking loudly. The dog later led neighbors back to its house—to the scene of two bloody murders.

At the crime scene, Marcia Clark scanned the walkway that led to Nicole's condo. While the victims' bodies had already been removed from the scene, signs remained that a violent struggle had taken place. Large pools of blood stained the walkway in front of the house. Blood drops and bloody shoe prints led away from the scene of the struggle.

Ronald Goldman was found murdered along with Nicole Simpson.

Near the victims, police had found a beeper, a key ring, a dark knit cap, and an envelope containing a pair of eyeglasses. A left-hand black leather glove, possibly worn by the murderer, had also been found on the reddened cement.

Clark took notes and asked lots of questions. She went into Nicole's empty house. (Sydney and Justin had been asleep during the murders. Officers had taken them to the police station.) Clark knew that every detail about the crime scene—no matter how small—could possibly give police a crucial piece of evidence. Police technicians gathered hair and blood samples from the scene. Scientists would analyze the samples in a laboratory.

Back at the District Attorney's Office, Clark began to build her case. She learned that several hours after Nicole and Ronald's bodies were found, police officers had gone to O.J. Simpson's home to continue their investigation.

The O.J. Simpson estate at 360 North Rockingham Avenue is about four miles from Nicole's condominium. At 5:00 A.M. on June 13, four officers arrived at Simpson's home. They buzzed the intercom and phoned the house, but no one answered.

They noticed a white Ford Bronco parked crookedly at the curb and saw what looked like blood on the door of the car. Concerned, the officers discussed what to do next.

Detective Mark Fuhrman, the youngest and most agile officer, was appointed to jump the high stone gate of the estate. Once he landed on the other side, he opened the gate for the other officers.

The detectives then woke Brian "Kato" Kaelin, an aspiring actor who lived in O.J.'s guest house. They also woke Simpson's daughter from his first marriage, Arnelle, asleep in her bedroom. O.J. was not home. He had flown to Chicago several hours earlier for a business meeting.

Kato Kaelin told the officers about a strange, scary "thumping sound" he had heard outside his room earlier that night. Detective Fuhrman searched the area around the guest house with a flashlight. There, between the wall of the guest house and a fence, Fuhrman found a right-hand black leather glove covered with blood. The glove matched the one found at the crime scene.

The officers then discovered more blood—a trail of drops leading from the parked Bronco to the front door of Simpson's estate. Later, after the officers had obtained a search warrant, they found more evidence inside Simpson's home. A pair of socks with blood on them lay at the foot of Simpson's bed. Officers took the socks and other evidence for scientific testing. If the blood at Simpson's home matched blood found at the crime scene, the police would have reason to arrest Simpson.

On June 16, O.J. Simpson attended his ex-wife's funeral with their two children. Though he had not yet been arrested, newspapers reported that Simpson was a suspect in the murder case.

The public O.J.—charming and friendly—seemed incapable of such a crime. Orenthal James Simpson, 47, had been a star running back with the Buffalo Bills. He later worked as a sports announcer and appeared in TV commericals and movies. But perhaps there was a side of O.J. Simpson that few people knew about.

According to police reports, friends, and Nicole's own writings, O.J. had threatened and beaten Nicole during and after their marriage. She had called the police many times asking for protection. She had written about the abuse during her divorce from Simpson two years earlier and had been photographed with bruises. Some of O.J.'s friends, and many of his fans, found themselves wondering—did O.J. kill Nicole and Ron?

Marcia Clark has a personal policy. She will not prosecute a defendant in court unless she believes he or she is "200 percent guilty." After careful review of the evidence, Clark had no doubt in her mind. She believed that O.J. Simpson had murdered Nicole Brown Simpson and Ronald Goldman.

By June 17, police had gathered enough evidence against O.J. Simpson to arrest him on two counts of murder. Simpson had cooperated with the police at first. But when officers arrived at an arranged meeting place to make the arrest, Simpson was gone. He had left a lengthy note. In the note, Simpson said that he had had nothing to do with his ex-wife's murder. Simpson's friend Robert Kardashian read the note aloud to the press.

Over the next few hours, Simpson and another friend, former football player Al Cowlings, led police on a low-speed car chase along Los Angeles-area freeways. From the cellular phone in his white Bronco (the same kind of car Simpson drove), Cowlings told police that Simpson was holding a gun to his head, threatening to kill himself. Cowlings said he was trying to talk Simpson out of committing suicide.

The bizarre event attracted hundreds of cheering onlookers, who lined Los Angeles roadsides and jammed overpasses. The "Bronco Chase Scene" was carried live on almost all television networks. Millions of people watched the chase, filmed by more than a dozen police and news helicopters flying overhead.

Eventually, Cowlings drove to Simpson's home, where Simpson surrendered to police. Cowlings was charged with aiding a fugitive and was later released.

Once in police custody, Simpson was questioned by detectives. They watched him closely. Did he appear anxious? Nervous? Angry? How strong was his alibi—his claim that he had been elsewhere when the crime was committed?

Bystanders cheer on Cowlings and Simpson in the Bronco.

Simpson said he was innocent. He thought he had been framed. Someone else had murdered Nicole and Ron, he claimed, and someone had planted evidence to make him look guilty. Simpson told the detectives that he had been napping at home when the murders occurred. Before the nap, he explained, he had gone out for dinner at McDonald's with Kato Kaelin.

Simpson hired a team of defense attorneys to help him. While lawyers on both sides of the case made their preparations, Simpson waited in jail. In July, after preliminary hearings, Judge Kathleen Kennedy-Powell declared there was enough evidence against O.J. Simpson to warrant a trial.

For more than a year, the Simpson case dominated the news.

Superior Court Judge Lance Ito was chosen to preside over the trial. Marcia Clark would be the lead prosecuting attorney. She would represent "The People" in what was to become "The Trial of the Century"—*The People v. Orenthal James Simpson.*

The case captivated the public from the start. People everywhere swapped opinions on the mysterious murders—and whether they thought O.J. Simpson was innocent or guilty. Schoolchildren and law students discussed the case in the classroom. Lawyers analyzed the evidence on television.

Many people tried to profit from the tragedy. Street vendors sold "Free O.J." T-shirts, buttons, bumper stickers, and other souvenirs. Tabloid newspapers printed far-fetched stories about Simpson, the victims, and others involved in the case.

News coverage was nonstop. Television, radio, and newspaper reporters set up equipment in front of the Los Angeles Criminal Courts Building. They soon nicknamed their media village "Camp O.J."

Whether she liked it or not, Marcia Clark had been thrown point-blank into the bright media spotlight. She was about to begin one of the biggest battles of her legal life.

The San Francisco Bay area—Marcia Clark's childhood home—in the mid-1960s

2

Practice Makes Perfect

Marcia Clark was born Marcia Rachel Kleks on August 31, 1953, in Berkeley, California. She was a pretty baby with big eyes and brown hair. Her parents were Roslyn Mazur and Abraham I. Kleks.

Abraham, an Israeli immigrant, was a scientist. He worked as a chemist and administrator for the U.S. Food and Drug Administration (FDA), a government agency that regulates the quality of food and medicine in the United States. Marcia's mother was a native New Yorker. In 1959 she gave birth to Marcia's brother.

The Klekses were a close family. They were religious Jews and felt a great kinship with the Jewish homeland of Israel. Politically, the Klekses were liberal Democrats.

From an early age, Marcia had boundless energy. She loved to dance. She especially enjoyed ballet, a dance form that requires grace, precision, and most of all determination. Marcia struggled to master the demanding ballet postures and movements. She didn't mind practicing difficult routines and dance steps over and over again.

She attended grade school in Foster City, a suburb of San Francisco. Her parents expected her to earn high grades and she did. Twice a week after public school, Marcia went to Hebrew school for religious lessons. One of her friends at Hebrew school was Roslyn Dauber. For fun, Marcia and Roslyn liked to sail on the San Francisco Bay in the Klekses' small sailboat.

As Marcia was growing up in the 1960s, social justice movements were sweeping the nation. African Americans were protesting racial discrimination in the South. Women were demanding equal pay and equal rights with men. College students were demonstrating against American involvement in the Vietnam War.

San Francisco became a hub for antiwar demonstrations. Protesters and peace activists flocked to the city. Though Marcia was still a young teenager, she felt like she was a part of the new movements. She, too, wanted to work for peace, equality among people, and justice.

"People who were growing up around San Francisco in this time thought they were remaking the world," Roslyn Dauber later said. Another schoolmate of Marcia's remembered, "We were these sixties kids. . . . We were going to save the world."

During junior high, Marcia had to leave her home and friends in California. The FDA transferred her father to its Maryland division. But before Marcia had time to adjust to a new school, neighborhood, and friends, her father was transferred again. Over time, the family lived in several states, including Michigan and Texas. Marcia and her brother had to learn to adapt to many different situations.

In 1968 Abraham was transferred to New York. The Klekses moved to a house on Queen Street in Staten Island. There, Marcia enrolled in the newly built Susan Wagner High School. She plunged into activities at her new school and earned top grades. Her favorite class was biology.

Marcia continued to study ballet. She also took up acting. She landed parts in several school plays, including *The Man Who Came To Dinner* and *Sabrina Fair.* Her teachers and classmates were impressed with her performances. Though Marcia was only a teenager, on stage she seemed much older. She played the part of a mature, sophisticated woman with ease. She thought about becoming a professional actress. She loved the limelight.

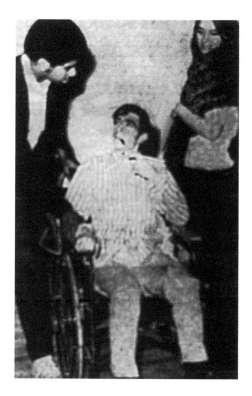

Marcia and two school-mates rehearse a scene from *The Man Who Came To Dinner.*

Three years after her arrival at Susan Wagner High, Marcia was once again uprooted. In January 1972, her father was transferred back to California. Marcia had no choice but to follow. She wouldn't receive her diploma with the rest of the senior class.

Back in California, Marcia had fun looking up old friends and seeing the sights of the San Francisco Bay area. She also looked to the future and made plans to attend college. In the fall of 1972, she moved again. This time, Marcia was on her own.

3

Attorney-at-Law

The University of California at Los Angeles (UCLA) is a large, sprawling school in southern California. It is known for academic excellence. There, Marcia Kleks signed up for a full schedule of classes.

She majored in political science, taking classes in government, law, and history. She also signed up for ballet and drama classes. Sometimes she still thought about becoming an entertainer.

She spent long hours studying, reading, and reviewing her class notes. She practiced ballet and rehearsed scenes for acting class. She also met an interesting man.

Gabriel "Gaby" Horowitz was not a fellow UCLA student. He was a professional backgammon player.

He was tall and handsome, with jet black hair and blue eyes. Like Marcia's father, Gaby came from Israel. He spoke with a thick accent. Well traveled and a flashy dresser, Gaby was different than most of the young men at Marcia's school. Soon, the two began dating.

Backgammon was a popular game in the 1970s, played for high stakes in private clubs throughout Los Angeles. Gaby often played at Pips, a star-studded headquarters for the backgammon fad. Many celebrities gathered at Pips to try their luck at the board game. Actors such as John Wayne and Lucille Ball reportedly lost thousands of dollars to Gaby at the backgammon table.

He excelled at the game and competed against some of the best backgammon players in the world. His gambling took him to clubs and casinos in other countries. When Marcia could find time, she accompanied Gaby on his trips. They enjoyed vacations in the Caribbean and Monte Carlo, a gambling resort in Monaco near the south of France.

By late 1973, Marcia had given up her sometime dream of becoming an actress and dancer. Instead she wanted a legal career. Upon graduation from UCLA, she planned to enter law school. She knew her grades had to be excellent. Though life with Gaby was exciting and glamorous, Marcia's primary focus was her studies.

Vacationing with Gaby Horowitz

Sometimes Marcia brought her schoolwork to Gaby's tournaments. There, she would pore over her textbooks while Gaby played at a nearby backgammon table. That way, Marcia and Gaby were able to spend time together despite their busy schedules.

After four years of hard work, in the summer of 1976, Marcia received her diploma from UCLA. She was eager to continue her studies. Just a few months later, she entered Southwestern University School of Law in Los Angeles.

Law school is both difficult and time-consuming. Students must memorize hundreds of laws and cases. Fortunately, Marcia had a superb memory. She also had excellent study habits and knew how to stay focused.

Law school was also expensive. To help pay the bills, Marcia took a part-time waitressing job at Lawry's steakhouse on La Cienega Boulevard in Los Angeles. Her pay was $2.50 per hour plus tips.

Marcia in Europe. Gradually, Marcia devoted less time to travel and more time to her studies.

She had plenty on her mind in the fall of 1976. But one thing topped her list—Gabriel Horowitz. On November 6, Marcia and Gaby were married. His mother, a dressmaker, sewed Marcia's white linen wedding gown.

The newlyweds honeymooned in Palm Springs. But, before long, Marcia's school and work obligations called her back to Los Angeles.

She and Gaby were both busy. Several times a week, Gaby gambled late into the night. Marcia needed her rest to do well in school, so she no longer joined Gaby at the nightclubs.

In 1979 Marcia received her law degree from Southwestern University. Before she could practice law, she had to pass the bar examination, a difficult test that all lawyers must take. Marcia passed the test with ease. She was eager to take the next step—to land a job as a lawyer.

A small but highly regarded Los Angeles law firm, Brodey and Price, was quick to hire Marcia. As a junior defense attorney, she would assist more experienced attorneys with criminal cases.

Soon after starting her new job, Marcia turned her attention to a painful personal problem. Her relationship with Gaby was in trouble. Because of their different work schedules, they rarely spent time together anymore. In 1980, after four years of marriage, Marcia filed for divorce.

Marcia's law school
graduation picture

Not long afterward, Marcia met someone new. She wasn't sure if she wanted to be romantically involved again so soon—but she definitely didn't want Gordon Clark to disappear from her life. Gordon was soft-spoken and down-to-earth. He worked as a computer programmer.

On October 7, 1980, just months after their first meeting, Marcia and Gordon were married in a simple ceremony. Both wanted to have children. But they agreed to wait until they were further along in their careers. They wanted to be financially secure before starting a family.

At first Marcia was excited about her work. But she soon faced a dilemma. As a defense attorney, her job was to defend her client—even if she believed the client was guilty. One such case would change Marcia's career.

James "Doc" Holiday was the leader of a Los Angeles street gang. He was charged with the attempted murder of a female companion. "Doc had lured this woman called Vicki D into a car," Marcia recalled later, "and then he stabbed her...and left her for dead—just a horrible, vicious crime."

Marcia's job was to defend Holiday, even though she believed he was guilty. One night Marcia was at home, writing a legal brief in which she asked the judge to dismiss the case. She knew she had a winning argument—the government's evidence against Holiday was weak. But, still, she thought her client was guilty. "I can't do this kind of work!" Marcia told her husband.

"Pick up your pen," Gordon replied. "We have to pay the rent." The thought of letting a murderer go free, simply because of a legal loophole, didn't seem right to Marcia. She was interested in seeking out truth and justice. That was why she had become a lawyer.

After almost two years at Brodey and Price, Marcia made the difficult decision to quit her job. Instead of defending criminals, she wanted to speak on behalf of victims of crime. Marcia's boss at Brodey and Price, senior partner Jeffrey Brodey, hated to see her go. Marcia Clark was a top-notch attorney. But he knew as well as Clark did that she was working for the wrong side.

"She was born to be a prosecutor," Brody remarked years later. "She always came from a very high moral plane."

4

Change of Focus

In 1981 Marcia Clark walked into the office of Los Angeles District Attorney John Van de Kamp. She was nervous, but it didn't show. She looked Van de Kamp squarely in the eye.

"If you don't hire me, I'm out of law," Clark said. Her voice was low and serious. "I can't do criminal defense . . . This is the only job I want."

Van de Kamp was impressed. Clark was more than willing to trade a high-paying career as a defense lawyer for that of a lower-paid prosecutor. She was just the kind of person he wanted on his staff. He immediately gave her a job as an assistant district attorney in Culver City, a small community near Los Angeles.

As one of only two district attorneys in the office, Clark had her hands full. She didn't have time to get used to the job slowly—she immediately took on a load of difficult cases, many of them homicides.

Over the years that followed, Clark acquired in-depth knowledge of criminal law. She learned about ballistics, the science that deals with the motion and impact of bullets from firearms. She fine-tuned her knowledge of "DNA fingerprinting." By testing DNA, genetic material from people's cells (such as blood cells), scientists try to match suspects and victims to evidence at a crime scene.

In 1989 Clark began working in the Special Trial Unit, which handled the district's most complicated, and often high-profile, cases. She loved the challenge of trial work. She almost always won her cases.

She found that working with victims' families was especially meaningful. Grieving family members appreciated how Clark was kind and understanding with them, but powerful and fearless in the courtroom.

In the summer of 1989, Clark took on one of her most difficult and celebrated cases. On July 18, 1989, Rebecca Schaeffer, a 21-year-old actress—costar of the television sitcom *My Sister Sam,* was shot in the heart and killed. The killer was Robert James Bardo, an obsessed fan. Though Schaeffer hadn't known it, Bardo had been stalking her for two years.

The morning after the murder, Clark met with Schaeffer's distraught parents, who had just flown to L.A. from their home in Portland, Oregon. She kept in close contact with the Schaeffers throughout lengthy pretrial hearings.

Actress Rebecca Schaeffer

"She wrote me a long letter before the trial telling me she was working like a dog on this case," recalled Danna Schaeffer, Rebecca's mother. "It was a letter on a yellow legal pad, just about how personally connected she felt to Rebecca. That's how she approached the case. She made us feel that she was working on our personal behalf."

As with most cases involving celebrities, the trial received much media attention. It was one of the first to be covered by Court TV, a cable station. After many months of hard work, Clark won the case. The judge convicted Bardo of first-degree murder and sentenced him to life in prison without parole.

The Schaeffers were very pleased. "They say nature favors the prepared mind . . . ," Danna Schaeffer said. "Marcia was brilliant at the trial. I worship that woman."

Also in 1989, Marcia's first child was born. Gordon and Marcia named the boy Travis. They hired a nanny to care for him while they were at their jobs.

Work and motherhood kept Marcia busy. She sometimes felt overwhelmed by all her responsibilities. And, again, Marcia's marriage began to trouble her. She tried not to worry and worked hard at her job, and at being a good parent.

In 1992 Marcia gave birth to a second son, Trevor. She loved being a mother. But she still didn't know if her marriage would last. Just a few months after Trevor was born, Marcia and Gordon separated. He moved out of their house.

Marcia wasn't certain she could manage alone. "That's what's funny," said a close friend. "Here's this incredibly strong, independent woman—in court— who was terrified of being on her own with two little kids to raise. She wasn't sure she could do it. But she's been amazed at finding out she can."

In 1993, Marcia's boss, Gil Garcetti, surprised her. After nearly 12 years of trying cases, Clark was promoted to supervisor. She would no longer have to face the long hours, legwork, and mountains of paperwork that went with trying cases. Instead, she'd have a desk job. She'd supervise other district attorneys who handled the court cases.

"I hated it," Clark said of her new job. "I begged them to let me back in the courtroom. I learned that all I wanted to do was try cases."

"Marcia was probably the first person in the history of the office to walk away from a supervisor's job and ask to go back on the line," said a friend, Deputy District Attorney Lynn Baragona. "Most people wouldn't want to make the financial sacrifice, and, as a single mom with two small kids, she has that very much on her mind. But she's got to be in court. That's why she's a prosecutor."

Just days after her return to trial work, Marcia planned a bridal shower for Lynn Baragona. The shower was scheduled for lunchtime on June 13, 1994. But, at the last minute, Marcia called to cancel the shower. Lynn was upset.

"I have to do this search warrant [at the Simpson estate]," explained Marcia. "It could end up being kind of big. I'll tell you about it later."

Afterward, Baragona said, "We laugh about that now. I guess it's a little bigger than 'kind of big.'"

Clark's colleague, Christopher Darden, questions a witness.

5

Trial of the Century

"Could you please get someone over here *now*," Nicole Brown Simpson pleaded with a 911 operator. "He's back. Please. . . . He's O.J. Simpson. I think you know his record. . . . He broke the back door down to get in before. . . . He's going nuts."

A chilling quiet settled over the courtroom as Marcia Clark played the haunting recording, a 1993 emergency 911 call, for the jury members. In January 1995, after months of hearings, legal proceedings, and jury selection, *The People v. Orenthal James Simpson* was finally underway.

Clark displayed photographs of Nicole's bruised face—pictures that Nicole made herself. As Clark played another 911 call for the courtroom, Nicole's sisters Denise and Dominique covered their ears and wept.

Clark faced the jury and spoke slowly and clearly: "The evidence will show that on June 12, 1994, after a violent relationship in which the defendant beat [Nicole Brown Simpson], humiliated her and controlled her, after he took her youth, her freedom and her self-respect . . . Orenthal James Simpson took her very life."

The small room in the Los Angeles Criminal Courts Building bulged with onlookers. The families of the victims sat together on one side of the courtroom.

O.J.'s family and friends assembled on the other. Cable viewers across the country watched the trial live on Court TV. Broadcast networks interrupted regular programming to present live coverage of the trial. Despite the millions of eyes watching her, Marcia Clark calmly took the jury, step-by-step, through a "chain of evidence" that she said linked O.J. Simpson to the murders.

She explained that on the night of June 12, limousine driver Allan Park arrived at the Simpson estate to drive O.J. Simpson to the airport. He was to take a late-night flight to Chicago.

There are two gates to Simpson's estate. One faces Ashford Street. The other is on Rockingham Avenue. Clark explained that when Park drove to the curb just north of the Rockingham gate, no cars were parked in the area. "No white Ford Bronco," she said. "And it was 10:39. That's very important."

Park decided to back up and try the Ashford gate. "At 10:40 he began to ring the buzzer," Clark said. "You could hear it sound but there was no answer. There were lights on upstairs—one light on upstairs. There were no lights on downstairs. It seemed . . . like no one was home . . . so he decided to page his boss and find out if perhaps the plans had changed. At 10:43 he paged his boss."

Clark then shifted the jury's focus to another scene at the Simpson estate. O.J.'s houseguest, Kato Kaelin, was on the phone with his girlfriend, Rachel, in his private guest house. At about 10:45 P.M., while Kaelin talked to his girlfriend, he heard three loud thumps.

"The thumps were so loud that a picture on that wall actually moved," Clark said. "Kato was alarmed. He asked Rachel, 'Have we had an earthquake?' When she said she hadn't felt any . . . he wondered if there might be a prowler." Clark explained that Kaelin then took a flashlight and headed outside. He noticed the limousine waiting at the gate.

Meanwhile, Park spoke to his boss on his car phone. "I don't think anybody's home," Park said. "What should I do?" His boss told him to wait a bit longer.

Park then saw Kaelin walking around the yard with his flashlight. "Almost simultaneously to seeing Kato in the side yard," Clark said, "[Park] saw a person, six-foot tall, 200 pounds, wearing dark clothing, African American, walk quickly up the driveway and into the front-door entrance."

She continued: "Immediately, as that person entered the house, the downstairs lights went on. Allan Park hung up the phone and walked over to the Ashford gate and buzzed again. This time, he got an answer. And [Simpson] said . . . 'Sorry, I overslept. I just got out of the shower. I'll be down in one minute.'"

Clark then explained how Simpson came out of the house with baggage in his hands. Kato Kaelin noticed that a small, dark duffel bag sat near Simpson on the ground. While Kaelin helped Simpson load his luggage into the limo, he talked about the strange noises he had heard. But Simpson, according to Kaelin, seemed "relatively unconcerned."

"While they were loading the bags," Clark continued, "Kato offered to get that small, dark bag on the grass and put it in the car for the defendant. Unlike any of the other bags, the defendant said, 'No, no, no. I'll go get it.'" Simpson then picked up the bag and put it in the car. At approximately 11:15 P.M., he and Park left for the airport.

Judge Ito presided over the complex and lengthy trial.

Clark then talked about Simpson's behavior during the ride to the airport. Park saw Simpson shuffling through his bags in the passenger seat, Clark explained, but couldn't tell exactly what Simpson was doing. "They arrived at the airport at 11:30," said Clark, "and that small, dark bag that the defendant insisted on putting in the car himself was never seen again after the defendant left for Chicago."

Clark suggested to the jury that Simpson had something hidden—possibly a murder weapon or other evidence—inside the small bag. Why would the bag completely disappear? she asked the jury.

She continued through a precise and detailed timeline: "Now, at this point we know the following. . . . Kato last saw the defendant at 9:35 . . . after they'd come back from McDonald's. Forty minutes later, at 10:15, we hear Nicole's dog barking that loud, insistent bark, that went on and on."

According to the prosecution's theory, O.J. Simpson had murdered Nicole Simpson and Ron Goldman between 9:35 and 10:15 P.M. "When Allan Park drove to Rockingham and saw that the defendant's Bronco was not there at the Rockingham gate, it was 10:39," explained Clark. "We know that the defendant had not yet returned home."

Clark pointed out that the drive between O.J.'s house and Nicole's condo took roughly six minutes. She said: "So, at 9:35, last sight of the defendant.

Forty minutes later, at 10:15 . . . Nicole's dog is barking. At 10:45, half an hour later, we hear the thumps on the wall. This leaves us between 9:35 and 10:45 to drive from Rockingham to Bundy [Nicole's house] and back, a total of twelve minutes, which leaves him a full hour to commit the murders."

Clark then turned the jury's attention to photographs of the crime scene. The pictures, flashed on a large screen for all to see, caused an outbreak of emotion in the courtroom. One photo, taken of Nicole's lifeless body from above, showed her in a curled position, her hands outward as if to ward off the attack.

"Now, what you're not going to be able to see in these photographs, ladies and gentlemen, is the fact that Nicole Brown's throat was hideously slashed," said Clark. "And . . . the evidence will show that her murder took very little time to accomplish.

"The same goes for Ron Goldman," Clark continued as she showed the courtroom a photograph of Goldman's dead body, lying near a fence. Some viewers gasped. Goldman's father, Fred Goldman, bent forward and sobbed.

Clark shared her opening statement with her colleague, Deputy District Attorney Christopher Darden. He focused his words on Nicole and O.J.'s stormy and sometimes abusive relationship. Assistant District Attorney William Hodgman and Deputy

District Attorney Lisa Kahn, a DNA evidence expert, also assisted Clark in the courtroom. Behind the scenes, nearly 200 attorneys and legal assistants aided the prosecution.

Clark and fellow prosecutor William Hodgman.

For months, Clark and her team brought forth witnesses, experts, and physical evidence. They presented the results of blood tests. Both DNA and standard blood tests showed that blood drops at the crime scene belonged to O.J. Simpson. Tests showed that much of the blood in the Bronco matched O.J.'s, while one spot showed a mixture of blood from O.J., Nicole, and Ron Goldman. Blood from the glove found at Simpson's house matched the blood of the victims. Nicole's blood was found on O.J.'s socks.

But the defense had its own experts, tests, and witnesses. For each witness and piece of evidence presented by the prosecution, O.J. Simpson's defense team made tough cross examinations and counterattacks. The defense lawyers had a difficult job to do—and they knew how to do it well.

Attorneys Robert Shapiro (left) and Johnnie Cochran led
O.J. Simpson's defense effort.

46

6

The Dream Team

O.J. Simpson's lawyers were famous and experienced. The group included Johnnie Cochran, Robert Shapiro, and F. Lee Bailey. The press nicknamed Simpson's lawyers "the Dream Team."

"We certainly don't refer to *ourselves* as the Dream Team," commented Cochran. "We're just a collection of lawyers just trying to do the best we can."

Robert Shapiro had been Simpson's lead attorney at first. But Cochran, a longtime friend of Simpson's, soon took the driver's seat. Cochran had successfully defended other famous people, including musician Michael Jackson, in lawsuits.

When the trial was in session, Simpson sat with his defense team, often taking notes in a yellow legal pad. He never gave testimony. At night and on the weekends, Simpson was kept in jail.

The defense wasted no time in challenging the prosecution's "chain of evidence" theory. Shapiro argued that Simpson simply hadn't had enough time to commit the murders. Cochran argued that Simpson would have been covered in blood, and that police would have found much more blood in his home, had he been the one to slash the victims.

One witness for the prosecution had been Detective Mark Fuhrman. Early in the trial, Fuhrman explained how he discovered the bloody right-hand glove—the main piece of evidence that linked O.J. Simpson to the crime scene. But the defense lawyers doubted Fuhrman's story. They accused him of lying to the jury.

Because O.J. Simpson, a black man, stood accused of killing two white people, the trial was fraught with racial tension. Mark Fuhrman was known to be a hateful racist. A few years earlier, Fuhrman had made ugly slurs about black people in a taped interview with a screenwriter. Witnesses stepped forward and testified that Fuhrman was indeed a racist who hated blacks.

Armed with this information, Johnnie Cochran accused Fuhrman of planting evidence against Simpson. Cochran said that out of racial hatred, Fuhrman and other Los Angeles police officers had placed the bloody glove and socks on Simpson's estate to frame him for the crime.

Clark faced a tough opponent in Johnnie Cochran.

The defense also blasted investigators for "sloppy police work." Although tests on blood samples placed O.J. Simpson at the scene of the crime, the defense questioned the test results. Defense attorneys and experts argued that the technicians who had gathered and analyzed the samples had contaminated the evidence. Test results could not be trusted, the defense said.

The testimony and arguments went on and on, back and forth. Witnesses answered questions about tiny details in the lives of O.J. and Nicole Simpson. A sales clerk said that Nicole had once bought O.J. the same kind of leather gloves as those found by detectives. Finally, Christopher Darden challenged Simpson to try on the infamous "bloody gloves."

In a dramatic moment, Simpson pulled on one of the gloves—with great difficulty. He squeezed his hand into the other glove, barely, and held the ill-fitting gloves up for all to see.

Clark's team was alarmed and quickly tried to explain the tight fit. Simpson had tried the leather gloves on over plastic medical gloves, they pointed out, so of course the gloves were tight. Blood had caused the gloves to shrink, the prosecutors also argued. Finally, they said that Simpson had been acting when he put the gloves on, spreading his fingers to insure a tight fit.

The defense team was pleased with the demonstration. The poor fit proved that Simpson was not the killer, defense lawyers said. Johnnie Cochran created a slogan that he would repeat again and again. "If it doesn't fit, you must acquit," he told the jury.

When not sitting in the courtroom, the 12 jurors were sequestered, or secluded. Each lived in a private hotel room. Judge Lance Ito didn't want the jury to be swayed by rumors or media reports about the case. He wanted them to consider only information presented in court.

Simpson struggles to put on the leather gloves.

Security guards monitored the jurors' conversations and phone calls. They were not allowed to watch television. A tattered newspaper arrived at each juror's door every morning. All articles about the Simpson trial had been carefully cut out. The jurors were never photographed or shown on television. Their names were kept secret.

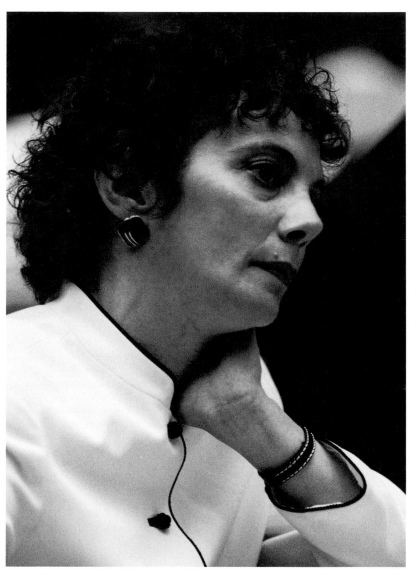

For Clark and others involved in the case, the media attention was relentless.

The other people in the courtroom, including Marcia Clark, had no such privacy. In March 1995, her personal life made the national news. Gordon Clark, who was now divorced from Marcia, had filed for temporary custody of their two young sons. In his legal statement, Gordon claimed that Marcia is "never home and never has any time to spend with [the boys]."

The custody battle angered many working women. Judy Mann of the *Washington Post* reported, "This is becoming a professional woman's worst nightmare: that the long hours she puts into a job to support herself and her family will be used against her and that she'll be judged by a harsher standard as a parent because she fails to fit the evolving working mother ideal."

"Let's imagine what would happen," continued Mann, "if a woman went into court and argued that she should be given custody of these children because her husband, a prosecutor, was working so hard that he only had one hour a day to give the children. She'd be laughed out of the courtroom, and the husband would be considered a hero for figuring out how to give an hour of his day to his children."

Under tremendous stress, Clark did her best to balance her personal and professional life. It wasn't easy. From the beginning of the trial, the press picked her apart. Tabloid newspapers printed absurd stories about her. Even well-respected publications focused on trivial matters such as her hair, makeup, and clothing.

She tried to make light of the situation. She joked to friends that she might say to Judge Ito one day, "Your Honor, I'd like you to grant this motion, and by the way, does this blouse look good on me?"

Simpson, here with Robert Shapiro, sat with his lawyers but did not testify during the trial.

In September 1995, after nine months of difficult and bitter debate, the attorneys presented their closing statements. Johnnie Cochran pointed at the jury. "Stop this cover up! Stop this cover up," he yelled, insisting that the police had framed Simpson. "If you don't stop it, then who?" Cochran then repeated, "If it doesn't fit, you must acquit."

Americans sat on the edges of their seats as the arguments drew to a close. Commentators wondered what role race relations would play in the jury's decision. The 12-member jury included 9 African Americans. Surveys showed that black and white Americans viewed the trial quite differently. *Newsweek* reported, "From the beginning of the trial, polling has consistently shown that. . . . blacks overwhelmingly side with O.J.'s defense, whites with the prosecution."

Had Mark Fuhrman planted evidence against O.J. Simpson? Some people thought he might have. Many African Americans said that they had seen police officers mistreat and harass black people. Fuhrman had even spoken on tape about abusing black suspects. The Los Angeles Police Department (LAPD) came under harsh attack.

In the prosecution's closing argument, Christopher Darden allowed that Mark Fuhrman was a racist. But, he told the jury, "You can't [wipe out] racism within the LAPD . . . or within the nation as a whole by delivering a verdict of not guilty."

Christopher Darden speaks on behalf of the prosecution.

Marcia Clark put in a final plea to the jurors. "Usually, I feel I'm the only one left to speak for the victims, but Nicole and Ron are speaking to you," she said. "[Nicole and Ron] are telling you who did it with their hair, their clothes, their bodies, their blood. Mr. Simpson, Orenthal Simpson, he did it. Will you hear them?"

On October 3, 1995, shortly after 10:00 A.M. Pacific time, millions of people all over the world stood transfixed at television sets, awaiting the verdict. In New York City, crowds gathered in Times Square to watch the decision on giant outdoor TV screens.

The jury discussed the case for less than four hours before coming to a verdict. The foreman of the jury read the decision aloud: "We, the jury, find the defendant, Orenthal James Simpson, not guilty of the crime of murder..."

At a press conference following the verdict, Clark comforted Ron Goldman's parents, Patti and Fred Goldman (in glasses).

In the courtroom, O.J. looked both stunned and pleased. He mouthed "thank you" to the jurors. Johnnie Cochran hugged his associate and friend. The jury had found reasonable doubt that Simpson had committed the murders. The defense had won. Across the country and around the world, viewers stood divided—some delighted, some horrified.

Marcia Clark believed that racial controversy, beginning with Mark Fuhrman and emphasized by defense lawyers, had been devastating to her case. She wasn't surprised by the verdict, but she was angry. She believed that O.J. Simpson had gotten away with murder.

7

Words of Wisdom

With the Simpson trial behind her, Marcia Clark took a six-month leave of absence from the District Attorney's Office. She was able to relax at home and spend more time with her sons. Marcia, Travis, and Trevor live in the Los Angeles suburb of Glendale. Marcia's ex-husband Gordon lost his bid to win custody of the two boys.

Clark wasn't nearly through with the Simpson trial, though. With the assistance of author Teresa Carpenter, Clark set out to write her own account of the murder case. She signed a $3 million book contract with Viking Press.

She also did a series of speaking engagements. On November 14, 1995, after three standing ovations, Clark spoke before an enthusiastic crowd of 7,000 at a women's conference in Long Beach, California.

Clark won high praise from her audience in Long Beach.

She wasn't there to talk about O.J. Simpson. Instead Clark talked to the women in the audience about self-esteem. "It was at the trial that I learned once and for all to trust my own instincts," she said, "to look within for the final decisions . . . whether anyone gave me the stamp of approval or not."

60

She encouraged women to be more powerful and to realize how much power they already have. "If even one of you walks out of this room today," she said, "and goes back home, or to the office, and consciously begins to . . . pay attention to how you make choices and decisions independently, all the time, and you begin the process of gaining confidence, earning your own self-esteem—then I will feel that all the pain and the stress and the misery of this trial was well worth it . . . "

The audience began to clap, but Clark hadn't quite finished her thought. "And, yes, even worth the ridiculous news coverage of my hair."

\\\\   \\\\   \\\\

Marcia Clark didn't plan to become famous. Her only goal was to do the work she did best. But after the "Trial of the Century," Clark found that her celebrity status gave her opportunities. "I want to use it [fame] to speak out about issues of social importance," she says. Whether Marcia Clark appears on a speaker's podium, on television, or in a courtroom, her role remains the same: She is a voice for the victims.

Index

ABOUT THE AUTHOR

Katherine Krohn, a graduate of the University of Michigan, writes biographies for young readers, news articles, and fiction. She has also written and produced an award-winning cable television series. She lives in Eugene, Oregon.

photo by Lou White

ACKNOWLEDGMENTS

Photographs used with permission of Reuters/Louis Raynor/Archive Photos: p. 1; Ken Kwok, Press Telegram: pp. 2, 60; Reuters/Corbis-Bettmann: pp. 6, 44, 46, 54; Darlene Hammond/Archive Photos: p. 9; AP/Wide World Photos: p. 10; Reuters/Sam Mircovich/Archive Photos: pp. 15, 36, 51, 52, 56; Reuters/Bettmann: p. 16; Archive Photos/Gerald French: p. 18; Staten Island Advance/Robert Parsons: p. 22; Media Associates: pp. 25, 26; Southwestern University School of Law: p. 28; Hollywood Book and Poster: p. 33; Reuters/Blake Sell/Archive Photos: pp. 38, 62; Reuters/Lee Celano/Archive Photos: p. 41; Archive Newsphotos/Steve Grayson Pool/Consolidated: p. 49; Reuters/David Sprague/Archive Photos: p. 57.

Front cover: Reuters/Lee Celano/Archive Photos